Teen Cookbook

A Cookbook to Easy and Delicious Recipes for Teens

By

Angel Burns

License Notices

This book or parts thereof might not be reproduced in any format for personal or commercial use without the written permission of the author. Possession and distribution of this book by any means without said permission is prohibited by law.

All content is for entertainment purposes and the author accepts no responsibility for any damages, commercially or personally, caused by following the content.

Table of Contents

Introduction

Do you want to cook your favorite dishes but can't find the right recipe? We have the answer! This book contains more than 50 recipes that are perfect for kids. They're easy, delicious, and kid-friendly. Plus, there are pictures for each recipe so you can see what the dish should look like when it is finished. Let us help you find your next family favorite!

This is not your typical cookbook. Sure, there are recipes for dishes like cake and cookies, but there are also recipes for a few more exotic things, like chicken curry and red bean ice cream. And this book does not just have food-related items. Instead of boring things like gift-wrapping or making a turkey sandwich, this book covers things that you may be looking for to have a successful school year, such as picking classes that will be fun or which clothes you should wear if it's cold outside. In a nutshell, this book is designed to help you be a better teen.

Benefits:

There are many benefits of learning how to cook. First and foremost, it saves you money. While it is true that there are some cheap ways to eat, most people are now aware that fast food is terrible for their health, tastes terrible, and can be very bad for your wallet. Cooking healthy food is much cheaper than eating out. It can also be a great way to meet new people because most communities have a monthly cookbook swap where you can meet other cooks who love cooking as much as you do. There is also the self-satisfaction of knowing you made something that tastes great.

How to Get Started:

Even if you don't have experience in cooking, it is easy to start making your food. All you need is a few supplies and some time. You will need some basic ingredients and utensils. There are two main basic items that you need, a stove and a refrigerator. It is worth investing in both of these because they will last a long time and it can be very difficult to cook without them. The other thing you need is a cookbook. Start with a simple recipe like eggs and toast and try to make it as good as possible. After that success, move on to something more difficult, but if you do not love it, then stop cooking and try again later.

Be an adventurous eater.

Try new things when you can. As you're eating, think about the look, smell, taste, and texture of the food. If you don't like something, try it again, in a different form. I think okra is slimy, but I like fried okra. There are a lot of chocolate cakes; find one you love, and explore what it is that sets it apart from the others. Never write off a food after one try!

Breakfast Recipes

Some people cannot function until they have had breakfast, so this section is devoted to that meal. These recipes are easy to make and taste great. Many health experts believe breakfast is the most important meal of the entire day. Before heading out for a busy day of school, work, sports—or even just some fun with your friends or family—eat a good breakfast full of vitamins, minerals, and protein. It will help give you the energy to power right through the day!

Tropical Morning Milk Shake

This is a great breakfast for a hot summer day when you just want something lighter. All you need is milk, ice cream, chopped pineapple or another fruit of your choice, sugar, and salt.

Servings: 1-2

Preparation Time: 5 minutes

Ingredients:

- 1 Banana, Peeled
- 1 c. Unsweetened Vanilla Almond Milk
- 1 c. Unsweetened Coconut Water
- ¼ c. Pineapple Juice
- ¼ tsp. Ground Cinnamon
- ½ tsp. Vanilla Extract
- Handful of Ice

Instructions:

Place all the ingredients in a blender. (Remember to keep it unplugged until the lid is on and you're ready to hit the button.) Blend on high for 30 seconds. Turn off—and unplug— the blender, and then pour your milkshake into a glass (or two) and enjoy!

Seedy Parfait

This is a nice refreshing breakfast or snack. Packed with protein, this power breakfast makes boxed cereals look like cardboard and fluff. When this homemade granola is added to yogurt, a delicious parfait is a result.

Servings: 4

Preparation Time: 30 minutes

Ingredients:

- 3 c. Oats, Rolled
- 1/3 c. Unprocessed, Coarse Bran
- 1/3 c. Sesame Seeds
- 1/3 c. Raw Hulled Sunflower Seeds (See Note)
- ½ c. Honey or Maple Syrup
- 1 c. Coarsely Chopped Pecans or Walnuts
- ¼ tsp. Ground Allspice
- ¼ tsp. Ground Cinnamon
- 2 c. Mixed Raisins, Dried Cranberries, And Chopped Pitted Dates
- ½ c. Wheat Germ, Toasted
- 3 c. Yogurt of Your Choice

Instructions:

Preheat your oven to attain 350 degrees F.

Using a bowl, combine the oats, bran, sesame seeds, and sunflower seeds. Spread the oat mixture evenly on a baking sheet and bake until golden brown for approximately 15 minutes. Leave the oven on.

In the bowl you used for the oat mixture, combine the honey, nuts, and spices. Add in the hot oat mixture and stir until well coated.

Return the mixture to the baking sheet, spreading it out into an even layer. Bake the granola, stirring every few minutes, until it is brown all over, about 10 minutes. Pay close attention while it cooks—it burns easily!

In a large bowl, toss the granola with wheat germ and dried fruit mixture and set aside to cool.

Place a spoonful or two of yogurt in a parfait glass. Spoon some of the granola on top. Alternate layers of yogurt and granola until you get to the top of the glass. Repeat the process in two or three more glasses, or save the leftovers in an airtight container to make more parfaits another day.

Mini Muffin Pizza

Who doesn't love pizza? This is a quick, easy, and fun breakfast. You can eat it for breakfast or as an afternoon snack.

Servings: 4

Preparation Time: 15 minutes

Ingredients:

- 1 English Muffin, Split In Half
- 1 diced Tomato
- 1 tsp. Olive Oil
- 1 slice Canadian Bacon, Diced
- ¼ c. Shredded Mozzarella Cheese
- A Few Fresh Basil Leaves, Chopped

Instructions:

Preheat the oven to 400°F.

Cover a baking sheet with aluminum foil. Place the muffin halves cut-side up on the sheet. Top both halves with diced tomatoes and drizzle the olive oil on top. Add the Canadian bacon pieces and sprinkle the cheese on top.

Bake the pizzas for 10 to 12 minutes, until the cheese has melted and is starting to brown. Finally, carefully remove the pizzas from the oven, sprinkle the basil on top, and enjoy!

High-Rise Hero

Who said sandwiches are only for lunch? Why not build a breakfast sandwich? You can add whatever you want to it, which is why the ingredients list has so many choices! It tastes like a sandwich but without the bread. Also, if you don't like pizza, this uses eggs in place of the tomato sauce.

Servings: 1

Preparation Time: 10 minutes

Ingredients:

- ½ tsp. Butter
- 1 Egg
- 1 Slice Swiss, Cheddar, Mozzarella, Or Monterey Jack Cheese
- 1 English Muffin, Hamburger Bun, Bagel, Or Crusty Roll
- Avocado slices, tomato slices, lettuce, mayonnaise, mustard, enough for topping
- 2 Slices Deli Ham, Turkey, Beef, Salami, Or Chicken

Instructions:

In a skillet, melt the butter over medium heat.

Crack the egg into the skillet and fry for 2 to 3 minutes, flipping the egg halfway through cooking so the yolk breaks and the egg is evenly cooked.

Place your chosen slice of cheese on top of the egg for just long enough to slightly melt the cheese; then slide the egg and cheese onto the bread.

Add the rest of your toppings, and then sink your teeth into your own personal high-rise hero.

Deep-Dish French Toast

This is a unique take on French toast and by using the oven, you can cook both the bread and the egg at the same time. This works by baking one piece of bread at a time in muffin tins. This is a very rich breakfast, so don't plan to make it often. However, when you do, enjoy every second of it. Since this dish must sit in the refrigerator overnight, plan to start the night before.

Servings: 2-3

Preparation Time: 45 minutes

Ingredients:

- 2 tbsp. Plus 1 Tsp. Butter
- ⅔ C. Packed Dark Brown Sugar
- 2 tbsp. Honey
- 1½ C. Milk
- 1 Tsp. Vanilla Extract
- ¼ Tsp. Salt
- 1 Tsp. Orange Flavoring
- Grated Zest Of ½ Orange
- 3 Eggs
- 6 Thick Slices Bread
- 6 Tbsp. Frozen Whipped Topping (Such as Cool Whip), Thawed
- 2 Tbsp. Finely Chopped Pecans
- 6 Orange Slices

Instructions:

Grease the bottom of the baking dish (about 13-by-9-inch) with 1 tsp. of the butter.

In a small saucepan, combine the remaining 2 tablespoons butter, brown sugar, and honey. Cook over medium-high heat, stirring continuously so the mixture doesn't burn, until it is bubbling and the sugar has dissolved, about 5 minutes.

Carefully pour the mixture into the prepared baking dish, spreading it evenly, and then set it aside to cool.

In a large bowl, combine the milk, vanilla, salt, orange flavoring, orange zest, and eggs. Stir together with a whisk.

Dip one slice of bread in the milk mixture and lay it in the baking dish on top of the cooled butter-sugar mixture. Repeat this process with the remaining bread. Pour any leftover milk mixture on top of the slices. Cover your dish and allow to refrigerate overnight.

Once you wake up, preheat your oven to attain 350 degrees F. Uncover the baking dish and slide it into the oven. Bake until the bread is lightly browned for about 30 minutes. Remove the French toast from the oven and top each slice with some of the whipped topping and pecans, along with a slice of orange.

Cantaloupe Bowls

Nature provides the bowl for this refreshing breakfast or snack packed with any type of berries you like. Feel free to use raspberries, blackberries, blueberries, strawberries, or a combination of them all. This is really easy to make and tastes delicious.

Servings: 2

Preparation Time: 10 minutes

Ingredients:

- 1 large cantaloupe
- 1 c. plain Greek yogurt
- ½ c. fresh berries
- 1 c. granola

Instructions:

Slice the cantaloupe in half along the widest point. Cut about ½ inch off the bottom of each cantaloupe half so that each bowl rests flat on a plate. Scoop out the seeds with a spoon.

Add ½ cup of the yogurt to the center of each cantaloupe half. Top with fresh berries and granola.

Impossible Quiche

You might have thought quiche was a tricky technical dish until now. This quiche whips up fast and is cooked in the microwave! This is an egg recipe that uses eggs out of a can as the main ingredient.

Servings: 4

Preparation Time: 21 minutes

Ingredients:

For the crust

- ½ c. vegetable oil
- 2 tbsp. milk
- 1½ c. flour
- 1 tsp. salt
- 2 tbsps. soy sauce

For the filling

- 3 eggs
- ½ c. half-and-half
- ½ tsp. hot sauce
- 1 c. grated mozzarella cheese
- 1 (6 oz.) can French fried onion rings

Instructions:

To make the crust

In an 8-inch microwave safe pie dish, combine the oil, milk, flour, and salt. Working with your hands, mix the ingredients until you have a dough you can press into the pan to form the pie crust. Brush the crust with the soy sauce.

To make the filling

In a medium mixing bowl, combine the eggs, half-and-half, and hot sauce. Beat the mixture until well combined.

Add the cheese to the top of the pie crust. Pour the egg mixture over the cheese. Sprinkle with the onion rings. Set the microwave to 50 percent power and cook the quiche for 11 minutes, until it is set.

Gluten Free French Toast Casserole

This is a very easy and yummy recipe. It is a variation of the traditional French toast and it is great for breakfast or dessert. This is one of my go-to recipes, whether I have a company or I just want a special but easy breakfast.

Servings: 6

Preparation Time: 12 hours (refrigeration) & 45 minutes

Ingredients:

- 4 oz. cream cheese
- 4 large eggs
- ¾ c. milk
- ⅔ c. half-and-half
- ¼ c. maple syrup
- 1 tsp. vanilla extract
- ½ tsp. salt
- 1 (15 oz.) loaf gluten-free cinnamon raisin bread, cubed

Instructions:

Blend the cream cheese, eggs, milk, half-and-half, maple syrup, vanilla, and salt in a blender until fully combined and smooth.

Grease an 8-by-8-inch baking pan. Place the bread in an even layer in the pan, then put the egg mixture over the bread. Press the bread down to soak up the egg mixture. Cover the pan with aluminum foil and refrigerate overnight.

In the morning, preheat the oven to 350°F. Remove the aluminum foil and place the pan in the oven on the center rack. Bake for 45 minutes, or until golden brown.

Microwave Egg Casserole

This is another quick, easy, and tasty recipe. This uses an egg mold to make a larger portion, but if you don't have one, just make it in two batches.

Servings: 2

Preparation Time: 20 minutes

Ingredients:

- 6 slices bacon
- 1½ tbsp. butter
- ¼ c. chopped green pepper
- 4 eggs
- ½ c. cream of mushroom soup

Instructions:

Place the bacon on a microwavable plate and cover it with a paper towel. Place it in the microwave and cook on high for 7 minutes.

In a small microwavable dish, add the butter and green pepper. Cook in the microwave on high for 1 minute.

Beat the eggs and the soup together. Add the butter and green pepper to the egg mixture and stir to combine. Pour the mixture into a microwavable dish and cook on medium-high for 5 minutes, stirring often. Let it rest for 1 minute, and then sprinkle it with bacon.

Pineapple Coconut Pancakes

This is another unique breakfast that has the flavor of dessert but uses pancakes as the main element. This is also easy to make and can be made the night before, so you don't have to do much in the morning.

Servings: 4

Preparation Time: 5 minutes

Ingredients:

- 1 c. pancake mix
- 4 tbsp. butter, divided
- ¼ c. coconut milk
- ¼ c. pineapple chunks, canned
- ½ c. reserved pineapple syrup
- ⅓ c. maple syrup
- coconut flakes (sweeten), for garnish

Instructions:

In a mixing bowl, combine the pancake mix, pineapple syrup, and coconut milk. Stir to mix well.

Melt 1 tablespoon of the butter in a pan over medium-low heat. For a single pancake, pour ⅓ cup of your batter to a hot pan, pouring to form a "puddle." You need to press 6 to 8 pineapple chunks into your batter and allow your pancake to cook until it starts bubbling or for about 1 minute. Using a spatula, flip your pancake slowly so that your pineapple chunks won't be misplaced. Cook the other side for 1 minute. You can set more than one pancake to the pan, but ensure you keep enough spacing between the pancakes. Do the same for the remaining batter.

Plate the pancakes and serve with a topping of warm maple syrup together with a garnish of pineapple and toasted coconut.

Preserves and Cream Biscuits

This is a traditional English breakfast that is easy to make and tastes great. You can use any preserves you like for this recipe. These sweet biscuits are fun to make and a treat to eat. I love them fresh out of the oven, but they're also delicious the next day. Try these with any type of preserves you like.

Servings: 6

Preparation Time: 30 minutes

Ingredients:

- 1 c. heavy (whipping) cream
- 3 c. pancake and baking mix (such as Bisquick)
- ¼ c. preserves
- 2 tbsp. cream cheese, softened
- 2 tsp. sugar

Instructions:

Preheat the oven to 400°F. Very lightly grease a cookie sheet or 13-by-9-by-2-inch baking dish.

In a large bowl, combine the cream with the baking mix just until moistened; it will be more dry than wet. Lightly flour a flat surface, such as a cutting board, and turn the dough onto it. Knead the dough about 10 times by pushing the dough away from you with the heel of your hand, and then reshaping it into a ball and repeating.

Using a rolling pin, roll the dough into a ½-inch thick rectangle. Use a 2-inch round cutter and cut out the biscuits. Place the cut biscuits onto the prepared pan. Press the rounded side of a teaspoon into the top of each biscuit, making an indentation in the center.

In a small bowl, combine the preserves and cream cheese and mix by hand or with an electric mixer until smooth and well combined. Drop a teaspoon of filling into the indentation on each biscuit. Sprinkle the tops with sugar.

Place the prepared biscuits on the center oven rack and bake for 12 to 15 minutes, or until golden brown. They are best served warm. Do NOT freeze them. Leftover biscuits can be placed in an airtight container in the refrigerator for up to 2 days.

Cheesy Microwave Scramble

This recipe is great for breakfast, lunch, or dinner. It is a variation of scrambled eggs that also has cheese. That makes for one delicious dish. Ready in less than 10 minutes, this light and fluffy egg dish is perfect for busy mornings. Plus, you can easily customize it to fit your tastes with your favorite pre-cooked veggies or breakfast meats.

Servings: 1

Preparation Time: 7 minutes

Ingredients:

- Nonstick cooking spray, for coating the mug
- 2 large eggs
- 1 tbsp. milk
- 1 tbsp. grated Cheddar cheese
- ⅛ tsp. table salt
- Pinch ground black pepper

Instructions:

Spray the inside of a large microwave-safe mug with nonstick cooking spray. You'll want to make sure the mug is covered thoroughly so the egg doesn't stick.

Crack the eggs into the prepared mug and add the milk. Using a fork, mix until there are no more streaks of yolk or white, which is how you know it's well blended. Don't get too hung up on this, though—you're making a mug scramble, so it doesn't have to be perfect.

Add the cheese to the mug and season with the salt and pepper. Using a fork, stir until thoroughly combined. Microwave on high for 40 seconds.

Carefully remove the mug from the microwave—it may be hot—and stir the eggs with the fork.

Return the mug to the microwave and cook on high for 20 seconds.

Carefully remove the mug from the microwave and stir again.

Return the mug to the microwave and cook on high for 10 to 20 more seconds, or until the eggs have cooked through.

The Perfect Omelet

The key to mastering the omelet is to keep the eggs moving in the pan. You want to consistently move the liquid egg mixture to the edges of the omelet so it can cook properly.

Servings: 1

Preparation Time: 15 minutes

Ingredients:

- 2 large eggs
- 1 tbsp. unsalted butter
- 2 tbsp. milk
- ¼ tsp. table salt
- Pinch ground black pepper

Instructions:

In a large bowl, whisk the eggs until they turn pale yellow in color.

Heat a 10-inch nonstick skillet over medium-low heat.

Once the skillet is hot, add the butter.

To the eggs, add the milk, salt, and pepper. Whisk again until the mixture is frothy.

Pour the egg mixture into the skillet. Do not stir the eggs. Let them sit for about 1 minute, or until the bottom of the egg mixture starts to set up and become semi-solid.

Starting on one side, using a rubber spatula, gently push the semi-set eggs toward the center of the skillet. Allow the liquid egg from the top to run onto the bare skillet (you may need to tilt the skillet slightly). Repeat this process, working your way around the skillet. When you're done, there should not be any liquid egg mixture on top of the omelet.

At this point, the omelet should easily move in the skillet. If it seems to be sticking, using a rubber spatula, loosen it around the edges.

Using a rubber spatula, gently flip the omelet over. If you need assistance, try using a wider plastic spatula (generally speaking, you should not use a metal tool on a nonstick pan. If your skillet is ceramic coated, you definitely shouldn't use a metal tool, because metal scratches the ceramic). Briefly cook the omelet on the other side, for about 1 minute. You don't want it to get brown.

Using a rubber spatula, lift up one side of the omelet and fold it in half. Remove from the heat. Carefully transfer the omelet to a plate.

Everything Bagel Avocado Toast

This recipe is very filling and tasty. Also, it is easy to make and can be eaten at any time of the day. There are so many flavor combinations you can make with this simple avocado toast. Try the suggestions I provided or experiment with your own.

Servings: 2

Preparation Time: 5 minutes

Ingredients:

- 2 bread slices of choice
- 1 large ripe avocado
- ¼ tsp. table salt
- 1 tsp. everything bagel seasoning

Instructions:

Put the bread slices in the toaster and toast to desired doneness.

Using a chef's knife, cut the avocado lengthwise, maneuvering your knife around the pit. Firmly grip both sides of the avocado and twist around the pit to separate the halves. Using a spoon, scoop along the avocado skin to remove the flesh and put it in a small bowl. You can also just squish the avocado flesh out of the skin and into the bowl, if you want. Discard the avocado pit.

Add the salt to the avocado and using a fork, mash it to your desired consistency.

Spread half of the mashed avocado onto each slice of toast.

Sprinkle ½ teaspoon of everything bagel seasoning on top of each slice of toast.

Cinnamon-Raisin Breakfast Couscous

This is a very easy breakfast that uses couscous as the main ingredient. It is cooked in the microwave, so you can make it in no time.

Servings: 4

Preparation Time: 20 minutes

Ingredients:

- 1¼ c. milk
- ½ c. dried couscous
- ¼ c. raisins
- ¼ c. chopped walnuts
- 2 tbsp. light brown sugar
- ½ tsp. ground cinnamon
- ⅛ tsp. table salt

Instructions:

In a medium pot, heat the milk over low heat. Stir often until small bubbles appear around the edge of the pot.

Stir in the couscous, raisins, walnuts, brown sugar, cinnamon, and salt. Cover the pot with a lid and remove from the heat.

Let the couscous stand for 10 minutes. Resist the temptation to peek— couscous really is this easy, and it just needs time to steam and absorb the water. The mixture will thicken as it cools.

Matcha-Pineapple Smoothie

This is a variation of the traditional smoothie. It uses matcha as the main ingredient, but you can replace that with any other type of green tea powder. Matcha, a green tea powder popular in Japan and China, is packed with antioxidants. If you find that the matcha powder gives the smoothie a bitter taste, you can add three or four more frozen pineapple chunks and blend again until smooth.

Servings: 4

Preparation Time: 5 minutes

Ingredients:

- ½ c. packed baby spinach
- 1 c. frozen pineapple chunks
- ½ c. vanilla Greek yogurt
- 1 tbsp. ground flaxseed (optional)
- ½ tsp. matcha green tea powder
- Milk, non-dairy milk, or water, as needed

Instructions:

In a blender, combine the spinach, pineapple, yogurt, flaxseed (if using), and matcha powder. Blend until smooth. Using a rubber spatula, scrape down the sides of the blender to ensure everything is blended.

If the smoothie is too thick, add milk, 1 tablespoon at a time, blending after each tablespoon, until the smoothie has reached your desired consistency.

Lunch Recipes

It becomes challenging to ensure your busy teen eats healthy; you need to ensure they take the lunch meal. Lunch meals are always harder to make. Since you have a lot of work to do during the day, lunch is usually just a salad or a sandwich. Here are some great lunch recipes that will give you the energy you need during the day.

Tortellini & Spinach Soup

This is a tasty soup that is easy to make. It uses tortellini as the main ingredient and can be eaten for lunch or dinner. This recipe is simple, with a broth enhanced by tomatoes providing the base. The fresh spinach and cheese tortellini make it special.

Servings: 6

Preparation Time: 25 minutes

Ingredients:

- 1 tsp. olive oil
- 2 cloves minced garlic
- 1 (14 ½ oz.) can diced tomatoes with juice, no salt added
- 3 (14 ½ oz. each) cans vegetable broth, low sodium
- 2 tsp. dry seasoning, Italian
- 1 (9 oz.) pkg. cheese tortellini, refrigerated
- 4 c. baby spinach, fresh
- Parmesan cheese, shredded, as desired
- Pepper, ground, as desired

Instructions:

In a large pan, heat the oil on med. Add the garlic, then stir while cooking for one minute.

Stir in the broth, Italian seasoning and tomatoes and bring mixture to boil. Add the tortellini and bring to a gentle boil. Leave a pan uncovered and cook till tortellini become tender, seven to nine minutes.

Add spinach and stir. Sprinkle as desired with Parmesan & pepper. Serve.

Korean Fried Rice

This recipe is a variation of fried rice. It includes kimchi and other Korean flavors, so it is great for a taste adventure. Top the bowls with fried eggs to complete the meal.

Servings: 4

Preparation Time: 35 minutes

Ingredients:

- 1 tbsp. oil, safflower
- 3 chopped scallions, separate green and white parts
- 1 tbsp. minced garlic
- 1 1/2 c. chopped kimchi, reserve the juices to serve
- 2 tbsp. pepper paste, Korean (also called gochujang)
- 4 c. rice, short grain, cooked and cooled
- 1 tbsp. sesame oil
- 2 tsp. soy sauce, low sodium
- Coarse salt, as desired
- 4 eggs
- Optional to serve: nori seaweed, sliced thinly

Instructions:

Heat large wok on high heat till quite hot, 2 minutes or so.

Add the safflower oil, garlic & whites of scallions. Stir while cooking for 1/2 minute, till fragrant. Stir in pepper paste and kimchi and cook for one minute. Add the rice, soy sauce and 1 tsp. of sesame oil. Season as desired.

Remove mixture from the heat. Sprinkle using 2 tsp. of kimchi liquid. Stir in green parts of scallions.

Heat the last 2 tsp. of sesame oil in wok on med-high. Crack the eggs in skillet and season using salt. Cook for four minutes or so, till whites have set and edges are golden brown. Yolks should still be runny.

Divide the rice in four bowls. Place an egg atop each rice bowl. Serve with the nori, as desired.

Homemade Chicken Nuggets

This is a very easy recipe that uses very few ingredients. It is great for a weeknight dinner or even lunch. These nuggets are baked rather than fried, so you can experience less guilt when you're munching on them. They're an easy recipe for your teens to prepare.

Servings: 4

Preparation Time: 35 minutes

Ingredients:

- 1 lb. skinless chicken breast meat, boneless
- 1 c. Japanese breadcrumbs (also called panko)
- 1/3 c. Parmesan cheese, grated
- Coarse salt, as desired
- 1 tbsp. oil, vegetable
- 1/2 c. all-purpose flour
- 3 lightly beaten eggs
- To serve: spicy ketchup or honey mustard dressing

Instructions:

Preheat the oven to 400 degrees F.

Cut the chicken in 2" pieces. Spread breadcrumbs on rimmed cookie sheet. Bake in 400F oven for six to eight minutes, till golden brown.

Transfer breadcrumbs to shallow dish. Add the Parmesan cheese & 1/2 tsp. of coarse salt. Use oil to drizzle and combine by stirring.

Place eggs and flour in two separate, shallow glass dishes.

Increase oven temperature to 450 degrees F.

Set wire rack on rimmed cookie sheet. Coat rack lightly with non-stick spray.

Coat chicken pieces in batches in flour. Shake off any excess. Then dip them in egg bowl. Dip last in breadcrumbs to coat. Place chicken nuggets on wire rack.

Bake in 450F oven for 12 minutes, flipping pieces when halfway done, till chicken cooks through. Serve the nuggets with dipping sauce.

Easy Tomato Soup

This is a simple recipe, and you can use the same recipe for the pasta if you have some leftovers. It also uses a lot of spices, so it has great flavor. Tomato soup is just the thing for lunch or dinner on cold winter days. It's an easy recipe that your teens will be happy to make once in a while.

Servings: 6

Preparation Time: 20 minutes

Ingredients:

- 1/4 c. butter, unsalted
- 1/4 c. flour, all-purpose
- 1/4 tsp. onion powder
- 1 tsp. curry powder
- 1 (46 oz.) can tomato juice, no salt added
- 1/4 c. sugar, granulated

Instructions:

Melt the butter in a large pan.

Stir in the flour, plus onion & curry powders till smooth.

Add the tomato juice & granulated sugar gradually.

Leave a pan uncovered and cook for four to five minutes, till heated through and thickened. Serve with croutons if you like.

Fresh Veggie Ramen Noodles

Ramen noodles have a bad rep for being unhealthy, but that's not always true. Throw out the seasoning packets they come with and cook them with chicken broth and vegetables. This recipe is made with ramen noodles but changes the flavor to make it more fresh and healthy. This recipe is great for lunch or dinner.

Servings: 4

Preparation Time: 25 minutes

Ingredients:

- 1 tbsp. olive oil
- 1 diced yellow onion
- 2 diced carrots
- 1 diced celery stalk
- 1/4 lb. trimmed 1/2"-cut green beans, fresh
- Kosher salt, as desired
- Ground pepper, as desired
- 1 (14 ½ oz.) can tomatoes, diced
- 3 1/2 c. chicken broth, low sodium
- 2 ramen noodle packets – break in quarters and discard seasoning packets

Instructions:

In med. pot, heat the oil in medium heat.

Add green beans, celery, carrots and onions. Sauté for five to six minutes, till soft. Season as desired.

Add broth, a cup of water and the tomatoes. Bring to boil.

Add the ramen noodles. Lower heat. Simmer for three minutes, till noodles become tender. Season as desired. Serve promptly.

Cheesy Tostadas

They taste great as made in this recipe. Your teens may also like to use tostada shells instead of tortillas or possibly add extra lettuce and make them in shells like those made for taco salads. If you like tostadas, this recipe is great. It fixes the traditional tostada but gives it a cheesy flavor.

Servings: 6

Preparation Time: 35 minutes

Ingredients:

- 6 x 8" flour tortillas
- 1/2 lb. sliced mushrooms, fresh
- 1 c. zucchini, diced
- 2 tbsp. canola oil
- 1 (16 oz.) jar salsa, chunky
- 1 (7 oz.) can drained corn, white
- 1 (16 oz.) can warmed refried beans, vegetarian style
- 1 1/2 c. lettuce, shredded
- 1 1/2 c. cheddar cheese shreds
- 2 peeled and sliced avocados, ripe
- 1 1/2 c. tomatoes, chopped
- 6 tbsp. sour cream, light

Instructions:

In a large skillet, cook the tortillas for a minute or two per side, till browned lightly. Remove from skillet and set them aside.

In the same skillet, add oil, mushrooms & zucchini. Sauté them till tender-crisp. Add corn and salsa. Cook for two to three minutes, till heated fully through.

Spread beans over tortillas. Top using lettuce, salsa mixture, shredded cheese, tomatoes, avocados & light sour cream. Serve.

Easy Pulled Pork

This recipe uses pork as the main ingredient. It takes a little longer to prepare, but it is worth it. The texture of the pork will be soft and easy to shred, and you can use any sauce you like.

Servings: 8

Preparation Time: 6 hours & 35 minutes

Ingredients:

- 1 chopped onion
- 1 tsp. oregano, dried
- 2 bay leaves, dried
- 1 minced chipotle in 1 tbsp. adobo sauce
- 1 (28-oz.) can tomatoes, crushed
- 1 (14 ½ oz.) can whole tomatoes, in tomato puree
- 2 tsp. Coarse salt
- 1/2 tsp. pepper, ground
- 2 3/4 lb. trimmed, crossways-halved pork shoulder, boneless
- To serve: 8 split sandwich rolls; pickles; coleslaw

Instructions:

Combine the onions, oregano, chipotle, bay leaves, tomatoes, puree, adobo sauce, kosher salt & ground pepper in slow cooker. Add pork. Turn it till completely coated.

Cover slow cooker. Cook on the high setting for six hours, till meat is tender enough to pull apart. Transfer the pork to large bowl and shred with forks. Return the pulled pork to slow cooker. Toss in the sauce. Discard the bay leaves.

Serve the pork with sandwich rolls, pickles and coleslaw.

Bacon Wrapped Stuffed Mushrooms

These are great to make with leftover bacon. They are filled with cheese and herbs, so they have a great flavor.

Preparation time: 20 minutes

Servings: 10

Ingredients

- 10 portobello mushrooms, washed
- 4 oz. Cream cheese, slightly melted
- 10 Strips bacon
- 6 Chives, washed and chopped
- 1/4 tsp. Garlic powder
- Olive oil

Instructions:

Slightly coat a pan using the olive oil. Set your pan on a stove on medium heat.

Add in the mushrooms and bacon. Cook for about 15 minutes.

Make your stuffing by mixing chives, cream cheese and garlic powder in a bowl.

Set the cooked mushrooms on a plate and stuff with the cream cheese mixture to the underside of the mushrooms. Wrap a single slice of bacon around each stuffed mushroom. Set together using a toothpick if needed.

Shrimp Casserole

This recipe makes the shrimp the star of the meal. It uses cheese and spices to make a delicious casserole.

Preparation Time: 1 hour

Servings: 6

Ingredients:

- 6 corn tortillas, sliced into strips
- ½ c. light sour cream
- 1 c. green salsa
- 3 tbsp. all-purpose flour
- 4 oz. grated Monterey Jack cheese
- 4 tbsps. freshly chopped cilantro, divided
- 12 oz. cooked shrimp, peeled and deveined
- 1 tomato, chopped
- 1 c. corn kernels

Instructions:

Preheat your oven to 350 degrees F. Arrange half of the tortilla strips in a baking dish.

In a bowl, mix the sour cream, salsa, flour, cheese and cilantro. In another bowl, mix the shrimp, tomatoes and corn kernels.

Top the tortillas with the sour cream mixture, and then with the shrimp mixture. Repeat layers. Bake in the oven for 40 minutes.

Dinner Recipes

Chances are that you will have some time to cook a full meal at least once a week. So, we have some great recipes to help you out.

You may eat most of your dinners with your family or friends. Now and then, however, you will find yourself alone at home or eating long before or after everyone else. In that case, making a dinner that serves four or more isn't effective or efficient.

Tropical Cheesy Ham

Dress up an old favorite with a new combo of toppings. This sandwich is easy to make, and you can make it with ham. This makes it a tasty and easy meal idea for the kids.

Servings: 1

Preparation Time: 10 minutes

Ingredients:

- 2 slices sandwich bread
- 3 fresh basil leaves
- 2 slices Swiss cheese
- 2 oz. deli ham, thinly sliced
- 2 pineapple rounds, thinly sliced
- 1 tbsp. butter

Instructions:

Layer one slice of the sandwich bread with a slice of your Swiss cheese, then the ham, pineapple, basil, and the remaining cheese slice; add the other bread slice to the top.

In a skillet with a lid, melt the butter over medium heat. Place the sandwich in the hot butter and cover the pan. Cook until the underside of the sandwich is toasted to a golden brown, 2 to 3 minutes. Flip the sandwich and cook the other side.

Remove the sandwich from the pan, let cool until you can pick it up, and enjoy!

One-Pan Hamburger and Veggies

Here's the perfect one-dish meal that has meat and veggies simmering together in harmony. This is a simple recipe that can be cooked in one pan. It makes the vegetables and meat flavorful because they cook together.

Servings: 1

Preparation Time: 20 minutes

Ingredients:

- 1 tbsp. olive oil
- 1 small onion, chopped
- 2 stalks celery, chopped
- 2 to 3 carrots, cut into small pieces
- 1/8 tsp. garlic powder
- 1/8 tsp. curry powder
- Salt and ground black pepper
- ½ lb. ground beef
- 1 zucchini, cut into small pieces
- Cooked rice or noodles, for serving (optional)

Instructions:

In a medium frying pan, heat the olive oil and combine the onion, celery, carrots, garlic powder, curry powder, and a little salt and pepper. Sauté over medium heat for 2 to 3 minutes.

Add the beef and cook for 5 minutes more. Use a wooden spoon to break apart your beef while cooking.

Add the zucchini, cover, and allow to cook for about 8 more minutes until the veggies have softened.

Serve as is or over rice or noodles for a larger meal.

Festive Fried Rice

This is a nutritious—and colorful—way to dress up some leftover rice that's sitting in the refrigerator. This recipe is a healthy version of fried rice that can be easily made. It only has seven ingredients and can be on the table within 25 minutes.

Servings: 1

Preparation Time: 15 minutes

Ingredients:

- 1 egg
- ¾ c. mixed frozen peas, shredded carrots, shredded zucchini, and sliced red bell pepper
- ½ c. cooked brown rice (leftover from another meal)
- 1 tbsp. water
- ⅛ tsp. soy sauce
- ⅛ tsp. garlic powder
- ⅛ tsp. ground ginger

Instructions:

Crack the egg into a small bowl, beat with a fork, and set aside.

In a small frying pan, cook the mixed vegetables over medium heat. As the veggies begin to soften, add the rice and water. Cover and cook for 2 minutes; then add the beaten egg. Stir the ingredients together and cook until the egg is cooked through, 3 to 4 minutes. Add the soy sauce, garlic powder, and ginger, and stir until combined.

Spaghetti for Singles

This is a meal that you can make at any night of the week. It is simple to make and warm and filling. Making spaghetti usually yields far too much for one person. Try this version instead. Fancy—and just right for one.

Servings: 1

Preparation Time: 50 minutes

Ingredients:

- Butter, enough for the pan
- 8 cherry tomatoes, halved
- 1 small clove garlic, whole and unpeeled
- ½ tsp. sugar
- 1 tsp. balsamic vinegar
- 1 tsp. olive oil
- Salt
- 5 oz. spaghetti noodles (about a large fistful)
- 1 tbsp. grated parmesan cheese

Instructions:

Preheat the oven to 375°F.

Lightly butter a small ovenproof dish, and put the tomato halves and garlic in it.

In a small bowl, combine the sugar, vinegar, and oil. Drizzle this over the tomatoes. Roast the tomatoes for 25 to 30 minutes.

Meanwhile, bring a medium saucepan of salted water to a boil. Next, add the spaghetti to the boiling water and then cook as directed on the package, usually 8 to 12 minutes, until al dente. Carefully remove from the heat and drain the spaghetti into a colander.

Pour the spaghetti into a serving bowl. Add the roasted tomatoes and toss; discard the garlic or squeeze out the roasted garlic clove from the skin, mash it, and mix it into the spaghetti. Sprinkle Parmesan on top.

Slow Cooker Chicken

It's hard to believe anything this good can be this easy, so find out for yourself. This recipe makes quite a bit of food, so you'll definitely have leftovers for lunch—lucky you! This recipe is perfect for a chilly night. It will make your house smell wonderful with its spices and is a simple way to make chicken.

Servings: 2

Preparation Time: 5 minutes

Ingredients:

- 4 frozen boneless, skinless chicken breast halves
- 1 (15.5 oz.) can black beans, drained
- 1 (15.5-oz.) can corn, drained
- 1 (15-oz.) jar salsa
- 4 oz. fat-free cream cheese

Instructions:

Place all of the ingredients except for the cream cheese in the slow cooker (yes, the chicken breasts really do go in FROZEN).

Cook on high for 4 to 5 hours. Then add the cream cheese, stirring it in so it melts, and let the dish sit for 30 minutes before eating.

Creamy Pork Chop Casserole

This is a recipe that will make your mouth water. The sauce is creamy and comfort food at its best. The great part is you can add any vegetables you want. This casserole features pork chops baked in a creamy sauce with potatoes and cheese and topped with French fried onions. If there are any leftovers, they pair well with fried eggs.

Servings: 6

Preparation Time: 1 hour 5 minutes

Ingredients:

- 1 tbsp. vegetable oil
- 6 (½- to ¾-inch-thick) pork chops
- Pinch salt, plus ½ teaspoon
- 1 (10¾ oz.) can condensed cream of celery soup
- ½ c. milk
- ½ c. sour cream
- ¼ tsp. freshly ground black pepper
- 1 (24 oz.) bag frozen hash brown potatoes, thawed
- 1 c. shredded cheddar cheese, divided
- 1 (8 oz.) can French fried onions, divided

Instructions:

Preheat the oven to 350°F.

Heat the vegetable oil in a large skillet over medium heat for 30 seconds. Add the pork chops and cook for 6 minutes, or until golden brown. Turn the pork chops over and cook for another 6 minutes, or until golden brown. Drain and discard the oil. Sprinkle the chops with salt and set aside.

In a large bowl, combine the soup, milk, sour cream, pepper, and the remaining ½ teaspoon of salt. Stir in the potatoes, ½ cup of the cheese, and ½ can of the French fried onions. Spoon the mixture into a 9-by-13-inch baking dish. Arrange the pork chops on top of the mixture.

Cover and bake the casserole on the center rack in the preheated oven for 35 minutes, or until the chops are done and the mixture is bubbly. Remove the cover and top the chops with the remaining ½ cup of cheese and half can of French fried onions. Return the casserole to the oven and bake uncovered for 5 more minutes, or until the onions are golden brown.

Easy Beef Stroganoff

Stroganoff is one of those comfort foods that you can make at home and it will taste just as good as your favorite restaurant. Stroganoff was one of my favorite dishes when I was growing up. Tender beef coated in a thick brown gravy over egg noodles is easy to make. It's sure to become one of your favorite dishes, too.

Servings: 6

Preparation Time: 35 minutes

Ingredients:

- 1 lb. egg noodles
- ¼ c. butter
- 1 garlic clove, chopped
- 1 c. chopped onion
- 1 lb. beef steak, cubed
- 2 c. button mushrooms, sliced
- 1 (10.5 oz.) can condensed beef broth
- 1 c. sour cream
- 2½ tbsp. flour
- Pinch salt
- Dash black pepper, freshly ground

Instructions:

Prepare the noodles per the package directions.

In a large skillet over medium-high source of heat, melt the butter. Add the garlic and onion and cook until the onion becomes translucent for 7 minutes. Add the beef and reduce the heat to medium. Cover and cook for about 12 minutes, until the beef is tender. Remove the lid, add the mushrooms, and cook until the mushrooms become wilted for about 5 minutes. Add the beef broth and bring it to a boil.

In a small mixing bowl, whisk together the sour cream and flour. Once the beef mixture is boiling, whisk the sour cream and flour mixture into the beef mixture and stir continuously until the sauce thickens. Add salt and pepper to taste. Serve over the prepared egg noodles.

Chili Con Carne

This is an easy homemade chili recipe. It's made with ground beef and the spices that you like. It can make for some great chili dogs and or toppings for nachos or baked potatoes. Chili con carne means chili with meat in Spanish. I add beans to my chili at the end, but some people feel that beans don't belong in chili, so I'll leave that up to you.

Servings: 4

Preparation Time: 5 minutes

Ingredients:

- 3 tbsp. vegetable oil
- 1 c. thinly sliced onion
- 4 tbsp. diced green bell pepper
- 2 lb. rump roast, cut in to ½-inch cubes
- 3 tbsp. chili powder
- ¼ c. cold water
- 1 c. boiling water
- 1 c. canned tomato juice
- ½ tsp. salt
- 2 tsp. granulated sugar
- 3 garlic cloves, minced
- 2 (15 oz. each) cans red kidney beans (optional)

Instructions:

Heat the vegetable oil in a large skillet over medium-high heat for 1 minute. Add the onion and green bell pepper and cook for 7 minutes, or until the bell peppers are tender and the onion is translucent. Add the beef and cook, uncovered, for about 8 minutes, until it begins to sizzle and brown.

In a small mixing bowl, combine the chili powder with the cold water and whisk to create a smooth paste. Set aside.

Add the boiling water and tomato juice to the beef mixture in the skillet, whisk in the chili powder/water paste until blended, and then add the salt, sugar, and minced garlic.

Cover the skillet, reduce the heat to medium-low, and simmer for 1 hour. Remove the cover and simmer for 30 minutes more, or until the meat is tender. Add 1 or 2 tablespoons of hot water if the mixture thickens before the meat is tender. Add the kidney beans (if using) and heat for 5 minutes.

Roasted Turkey

Who doesn't love a roasted turkey? It is filling and delicious. You can serve it with mashed potatoes and gravy or make sandwiches out of it the next day. It's easier than you think to prepare a roasted turkey with pan gravy and homemade cranberry sauce. Gather your family and friends and amaze them with a made-from-scratch Thanksgiving feast any day of the year!

Servings: 10-12

Preparation Time: 3 hours and 5 minutes

Ingredients:

- 1 (14 lb.) whole turkey
- 1 tbsp. salt

Instructions:

Preheat the oven to 450°F.

In a deep roasting pan, place the turkey, breast-side up. Sprinkle with salt and roast in the preheated oven for 1 hour. Using a spoon or baster, baste the turkey with the juices in the bottom of the pan, and then decrease the oven temperature to 350°F.

Roast the turkey for 2 hours more, or until the turkey is golden brown and cooked through. The temperature measured on a meat thermometer from the thigh should read 165°F.

Transfer the turkey to a platter and pour the juices into a medium mixing bowl. Be sure to scrape the particles stuck to the bottom of the pan into the liquid.

Easy Ground Beef Tacos

Whether for breakfast, lunch, dinner, or a late-night snack, tacos are always a good idea. The possibilities for toppings and combinations are endless, but some of my favorites are shredded Cheddar cheese, chopped tomatoes, shredded lettuce, sour cream, and guacamole. This is a classic! Serve with chips and guacamole or fresh salsa.

Servings: 4

Preparation Time: 20 minutes

Ingredients:

- 1 tsp. chili powder
- 1 tsp. all-purpose flour
- ½ tsp. cumin, ground
- ¼ tsp. table salt
- ¼ tsp. oregano, dried
- ¼ tsp. powdered garlic
- ¼ tsp. black pepper, ground
- ⅓ lb. ground beef
- 3 tbsp. canned tomato sauce
- 1 tbsp. water
- 4 hard taco shells or 6-inch soft corn tortillas

Instructions:

To make the seasoning mixture, put the chili powder, flour, cumin, salt, oregano, garlic powder, and pepper in a bowl. Stir to combine.

Place the ground beef in a skillet set over medium-high heat. Using a spoon, break the beef apart.

Add the seasoning mixture to the beef and cook for approximately 5 minutes, or until the beef is no longer pink.

Reduce the heat to medium. Stir in the tomato sauce and water. Cook for 7 minutes, stirring occasionally. The sauce will thicken slightly as it cooks. Remove from the heat.

Warm the taco shells according to the package directions.

Spoon 2 heaping tablespoons of taco meat into each shell and add toppings as desired, such as shredded Cheddar cheese, chopped tomatoes, shredded lettuce, sour cream, and guacamole.

Grilled Cheese Hot Dogs

It may seem odd to use mayonnaise on the outside of the sandwich. However, prepare to have your life changed: Mayo has a high smoke point, which makes it easier to get a crispier exterior on the bread without burning it. Toasty hot dogs inside a grilled cheese sandwich. Quick, easy, and totally worth the mess!

Servings: 2

Preparation Time: 15 minutes

Ingredients:

- 2 hot dogs
- 4 scallions
- 2 tbsp. mayonnaise
- ¼ tsp. garlic powder
- ¼ tsp. onion powder
- 1 c. shredded Colby Jack cheese, divided
- 4 bread slices of choice

Instructions:

Cut the hot dogs in half crosswise. Without going all the way through, cut each half down the middle, lengthwise—just cut them enough so that you can open the hot dogs like a book.

Trim the scallions by cutting ½ inch off the top and cutting off the root end. Cut the remaining scallions into thin circles.

Put the mayonnaise, garlic powder, and onion powder in a bowl. Stir to combine.

Heat the skillet in medium heat.

Put the hot dog halves in the skillet and cook for 2 minutes per side, or until they're slightly browned. Remove from the heat.

Divide ½ cup of cheese between 2 bread slices.

Place the flattened hot dog halves on top of the cheese.

Add the remaining ½ cup of cheese on top of the hot dogs.

Divide the scallions between the 2 sandwiches.

Place the remaining 2 bread slices on top.

Spread half of the mayonnaise mixture on the top of each sandwich.

Heat the skillet over medium heat.

Once the skillet is hot, carefully place both sandwiches in the skillet, mayonnaise-side down.

Spread the remaining mayonnaise mixture on the top of each sandwich.

Cook for 2 minutes, or until the bottoms are golden.

Flip the sandwiches and cook for 2 more minutes. Remove from the heat.

Chicken Enchilada Street Fries

Crispy fried potatoes topped with cheesy, chicken enchilada goodness. Ordinarily, "fries" are considered finger food, but you're going to need a knife and fork for this loaded dish. You're welcome.

Servings: 2

Preparation Time: 25 minutes

Ingredients:

- 2 oz. frozen French fries
- 1 c. shredded cooked chicken
- ½ c. canned red enchilada sauce
- ¼ c. sour cream
- 2 tsp. milk
- ¼ c. canned black beans
- ¼ c. canned corn
- 1 red onion
- ½ c. shredded Cheddar cheese
- 1 lime wedge

Instructions:

Preheat the oven according to the fry package's directions, usually around 425°F. Line a small rimmed baking sheet with aluminum foil.

Place the fries on the prepared baking sheet. Next, bake according to the package directions, usually about 20 minutes, or until crispy. Remove from the oven, leaving the oven on.

In a small bowl, combine the cooked chicken and enchilada sauce. Put the sour cream and milk in another small bowl. Stir to combine.

Drain the black beans and corn in a strainer, then rinse with cold water.

To finely dice the onion, start by cutting the onion in half from root to tip. Peel off the papery outside layer and a layer of onion underneath that. For each onion half, cut off the tip of the onion, but leave the root end intact. Cut each onion half in half again from root to tip. Place an onion quarter, flat-side down, on a cutting board. Make several vertical cuts from end to end, being careful not to cut through the root end. Flip the onion quarter onto the other flat side and repeat the vertical cuts, again being careful not to cut through the root end. Then cut the onion crosswise into small, even dice—the pieces should just fall off the knife ready to go. Set aside 2 tablespoons and store any leftover onion.

Switch the oven to broil.

Top the fries with the chicken mixture and spread the cheese over the chicken.

Top with the beans, corn, and onion.

Return the baking sheet to the oven and broil for 1 minute, or until the cheese melts. Remove from the oven.

Drizzle the sour cream mixture and squeeze the lime wedge over the top of the fries.

Oven-Fried Chicken Tenders with Honey-Mustard Sauce

These chicken tenders are so crispy and delicious that you won't be able to stop eating them! These crispy chicken tenders are incredibly easy to make and full of flavor. I usually make a double batch because they're great reheated (ideally in a 300°F oven for 5 to 10 minutes).

Servings: 2

Preparation Time: 30 minutes

Ingredients:

- Nonstick cooking spray, for coating the wire rack
- 1 tbsp. unsalted butter
- ¾ c. panko bread crumbs
- 1½ tbsp. Dijon mustard
- 1 large egg
- 1 tbsp. mayonnaise
- 2 tbsp. all-purpose flour
- ½ tsp. table salt
- ¼ tsp. ground black pepper
- ½ lb. chicken tenderloins
- ¼ c. honey-mustard dipping sauce

Instructions:

Preheat the oven to 400°F. Place a wire rack on a rimmed baking sheet and spray with nonstick cooking spray. If you don't have a wire rack, you can use the wire rack from a toaster oven.

In a medium skillet, melt the butter over the medium-high heat.

Add the bread crumbs and cook for 2 to 3 minutes, or until the bread crumbs turn golden. Remove from the heat. Transfer to a shallow bowl.

To make the batter, put the egg, mayonnaise, mustard, flour, salt, and pepper in a small bowl. Whisk until combined.

Using tongs, dip the chicken in the batter, ensuring the entire tenderloin is completely coated.

Place the tenderloin in the bread crumbs. Using tongs, press the crumbs into the chicken.

Place the coated chicken in a single layer on the prepared wire rack.

Transfer the baking sheet to the oven and bake for 15 minutes, or until a meat thermometer inserted into the thickest part of the chicken reads 165°F. Remove from the oven.

Serve the chicken with the honey-mustard dipping sauce on the side.

Bacon-Ranch Chicken

This is a great dinner recipe and you can serve it with rice or other veggies. It tastes like take-out chicken.

Servings: 4

Preparation Time: 5 minutes

Ingredients:

- Nonstick cooking spray, for coating the baking dish
- 2 boneless, skinless chicken breasts
- ½ c. grated parmesan cheese, divided
- ¼ tsp. table salt
- ⅛ tsp. ground black pepper
- ¾ c. ranch dressing
- ¼ c. sour cream
- 2 bacon slices

Instructions:

Preheat the oven to 375°F. Spray a 9-by-9-inch metal baking dish with nonstick cooking spray.

If the chicken breasts are thicker than 1 inch, using a meat mallet, pound them so that they're 1 inch thick.

Put the chicken breasts in the baking dish.

In a small bowl, combine ¼ cup of parmesan cheese, the salt, and pepper.

In another small bowl, stir together the ranch dressing and sour cream.

Sprinkle the parmesan cheese mixture evenly over the chicken.

Slather the ranch dressing mixture evenly over the chicken.

Top with the remaining ¼ cup of parmesan cheese.

Transfer the baking dish to the oven and bake for 20 minutes, or until a meat thermometer inserted into the thickest part of the chicken reads 155°F. Remove from the oven.

While the chicken is baking, cut the bacon into ½-inch pieces.

Line a plate with paper towels. In a skillet, cook the bacon over medium-high heat for about 5 minutes, or until crispy and browned. Remove from the heat. Using tongs or a slotted spoon, transfer the bacon to the prepared plate.

Once the chicken is out of the oven, switch the oven to broil.

Return the baking dish to the oven and broil the chicken for 2 minutes, or until golden and bubbly. Do not walk away because the chicken can burn quickly. The chicken is done when a meat thermometer inserted into the thickest part reads 165°F. Remove from the oven.

Top the chicken with the bacon pieces and serve.

Beef and Broccoli Stir-Fry

This span-friendly dish is filled with veggies, beef, and delicious sauce. This recipe has a rich, luxurious sauce. It's important that you remove the excess cornstarch from the beef before adding it to the skillet.

Servings: 2

Preparation Time: 20 minutes

Ingredients:

- 2 garlic cloves
- 1 c. broccoli florets
- ½ lb. flank steak
- 2 tbsp. cornstarch
- 2 tbsp. canola oil
- 1 tsp. grated fresh ginger
- ¼ c. low-sodium soy sauce
- ¼ c. water
- ¼ c. packed dark brown sugar

Instructions:

Press each garlic clove so it gets a little squished, then peel off the papery layer and cut off the root ends (the nubby side). Mince the garlic: Moving the knife blade in a rocking motion, run the knife over the squished cloves repeatedly. Use the knife blade to turn the pile of cut garlic a quarter turn every few seconds. Continue this until the garlic is cut into very fine pieces (minced).

Fill a medium saucepan with water and allow to boil.

On boiling, add in your broccoli and let cook for about 2 minutes. Remove from the heat. Drain the broccoli in a strainer.

Cut the steak into ¼-inch-thick slices. Put into a zip-top bag.

Add the cornstarch to the bag. Seal the bag, removing any excess air. Shake to coat all the steak in the cornstarch.

In a large skillet, heat the canola oil over medium-high heat until it shimmers.

Shake off excess cornstarch from the steak, and using tongs, add the coated steak to the skillet in a single layer. Cook for 1 minute per side. Remove the steak from the skillet.

Add the garlic and ginger to the skillet and cook for 30 seconds.

Add the soy sauce, water, and brown sugar. Bring to a simmer.

Add the steak and broccoli. Simmer for 1 to 2 minutes. Remove from the heat.

Poke Bowl

Learn how to make a quick and easy dinner bowl with tuna, avocado, and other toppings. Poke is a Hawaiian dish of marinated raw fish. Because the concept is similar to sushi, you have to get the freshest sushi-grade tuna you can find.

Servings: 2

Preparation Time: 1 hour & 10 minutes

Ingredients:

- ½ lb. sushi-grade ahi tuna
- 1 tbsp. low-sodium soy sauce
- 2 tsp. sesame oil
- 2 tsp. rice vinegar
- ½ tsp. honey
- 2 tbsp. mayonnaise
- ½ tsp. sriracha
- ⅛ tsp. table salt
- Pinch ground black pepper
- ½ cucumber
- ½ carrot
- 2 c. prepared instant rice
- ¼ c. shelled edamame

Instructions:

Cut the tuna into ½-inch pieces.

Put the soy sauce, rice vinegar, sesame oil, and honey in a medium bowl. Whisk to combine. (If you're using seasoned rice vinegar, start with ¼ teaspoon of honey and adjust to taste.)

Add the tuna to the soy sauce mixture and stir until evenly coated. You can let this marinate in a covered container in the fridge for an hour or more, if you wish.

In a small bowl, combine the mayonnaise, sriracha, salt, and pepper.

Peel the cucumber and cut into ¼-inch squarish pieces.

Peel the carrot and shred on the large holes of a box grater.

Divide the rice, tuna, cucumber, carrot, and edamame between 2 bowls.

Drizzle with the sriracha mayo.

Desserts and Snacks Recipes

Yes, it's the remarkable time of day known as . . . the Snack Attack! The symptoms often strike right around the time you get out of school and walk through the front door of your house. Thoughts of school, homework, friends, and chores all fade as you think about your increasingly demanding stomach. Lunch was eons ago, and dinner is just floating out there, unseen, in the coming evening hours. These recipes are sweet and tasty. They are perfect as a snack or as a delicious dessert. They each have their own unique flavor.

Ice Pop Paradise

This is a recipe for an ice pop that uses fruity flavors and fresh, fresh fruit. The Popsicles you get at the store often have more sugar and artificial flavorings and colorings than any other ingredient. You can make your own at home with fruit juice and fruit, which costs less and tastes better. Here is just one possibility.

Servings: yield varies based on size of molds

Preparation Time: 6 hours

Ingredients:

- 1 ½ c. Seedless White or Red Grapes, Halved
- 3 c. White or Purple Grape Juice
- 1 ½ c. Cranberry Juice
- Craft Sticks (Available at Craft Stores)

Instructions:

Drop 4 to 6 grape halves into each ice pop mold.

Combine the grape juice and cranberry juice in a pitcher; then pour the mixture into the molds almost to the top.

Insert a stick into each mold and place the molds in the freezer. Freeze for at least 6 hours, until solid. Before eating, pull out the molds and let them stand at room temperature for a few minutes so the ice pops will be easy to remove from the molds.

Sweet Potato Surprise

You already know that potatoes make tasty French fries. Believe it or not, so do sweet potatoes, and they have slightly fewer calories, too.

Servings: 4

Preparation Time: 5 minutes

Ingredients:

- 4 sweet potatoes
- ½ tsp. ground cinnamon
- 2 tbsp. vegetable oil
- ½ c. sour cream, for dipping

Instructions:

Preheat the oven to 450°F.

Wash the sweet potatoes and pat them dry. Halve each sweet potato lengthwise, and then cut each half into three long pieces. Place all the pieces in a large bowl and sprinkle with the cinnamon and the oil. Stir until they are evenly coated.

Place the sweet potato fries in a single layer on a baking sheet and bake for 15 minutes. Take the pan out and flip the fries over. Bake for 15 minutes more. Check the fries—if they are done, a fork should slide easily into them. If they are not quite done, continue baking for 3 to 4 minutes and then check them again. Remove the baking sheet from the oven and let the fries cool slightly. When they are cool enough to handle, serve them with the sour cream for dipping.

Popcorn Perfection

Popcorn has a bad reputation—but that's largely because of the heaps of butter and salt that many people add to it. Can you have your popcorn and be healthy, too? Of course! Just try this instead. The secret to this delicious and fun snack is the super-special seasoning.

Servings: 1-2

Preparation Time: 5 minutes

Ingredients:

- 1 bag plain microwave popcorn
- ¼ c. grated parmesan cheese
- ¼ tsp. garlic powder
- ¼ tsp. Cajun seasoning or cayenne pepper
- ¼ tsp. salt
- ¼ tsp. ground black pepper

Instructions:

Pop your bag of microwave popcorn, and then add all of the seasonings (if you don't want to dirty a bowl, you don't even need to take the popcorn out of the bag!). Shake the bag to coat the popcorn in the seasonings, and snack away.

Sweet and Salty Nuts

This is a healthy snack that is also the perfect game day food. If you can't decide which you like better—sweet? salty? —how about putting them together and ending the debate? This fast, protein-packed snack can give you the stamina for an afternoon of homework or a late night up with friends.

Servings: 2

Preparation Time: 40 minutes

Ingredients:

- 1 tbsp. butter
- 2 c. salted nuts (a mix of your favorites, such as peanuts, cashews, pecans, walnuts, almonds, or pistachios)
- 1 tbsp. lime juice
- 2 tsp. sugar
- ½ tsp. salt
- 1 tsp. chili powder

Instructions:

Preheat the oven to 300°F.

In a medium skillet, melt the butter slowly over low heat. Alternatively, microwave the butter in a medium bowl for 30 to 60 seconds to melt it.

Next, add the nuts and lime juice to the melted butter. Stir until the nuts are completely coated. Spread the nuts into a single layer on a baking sheet and bake for 35 minutes, until toasted. Stir the nuts a few times while they bake.

Remove from the oven, and while the nuts are still warm, sprinkle them with the sugar, salt, and chili powder. Stir well.

Bagel Bakes

These are a fun twist on the traditional bagel sandwich and they are super easy to make. This recipe adapts to your preferences. Feel like you need a sweet treat? Make the first version. Rather have a savory snack? Try the second.

Servings: 1

Preparation Time: 25 minutes

Ingredients:

- ¼ Tsp. Ground Cinnamon
- ½ Tsp. Sugar
- 1 Tbsp. Butter
- 1 Cinnamon-Raisin Bagel

Instructions:

Preheat the oven to 325°F. In a small bowl, combine the cinnamon and sugar. Set aside.

In a small skillet, melt the butter slowly over low heat. Alternatively, microwave the butter in a small bowl for 30 to 60 seconds to melt it.

Very carefully slice the bagel horizontally into four thin, round pieces. Using a pastry brush, coat the tops of the slices with the melted butter. Sprinkle the bagel slices with the cinnamon-sugar. Place the bagel slices on a baking sheet and bake for 10 minutes.

Remove the baking sheet from the oven, flip the bagel slices, and repeat the coating process on the other side. Bake for 10 minutes more and serve. Crunchy sweetness!

Strawberry Cupcakes

These cupcakes are a fun twist on the usual strawberry cake and are super easy to make. These cupcakes are so fluffy and pink, and they have a real strawberry taste. They're the perfect teen-prepared summer treat.

Servings: 16

Preparation Time: 3 hours 55 minutes

Ingredients:

- 9 fresh strawberries, large
- 1 egg
- 2 egg whites from large eggs, separated & at room temperature
- 2 c. flour, all-purpose
- 1/4 c. corn starch
- 1/2 tsp. kosher salt
- 2 1/2 tsp. baking powder
- 3/4 c. softened butter, unsalted
- 1 1/2 c. granulated sugar
- 3 tsp. vanilla extract, pure
- 1 c. room temperature whole milk
- Strawberry buttercream frosting, prepared

Instructions:

Preheat the oven to 350 degrees F. Line 12-pan muffin tin with liners. This cupcake recipe makes 16 regular-sized cupcakes, so you'll have extra batter for later.

Slice five strawberries. Pour into food processor and pulse till strawberries form chunky puree. Set the puree aside. Chop the remainder of strawberries finely and set them aside, too.

Beat 3 large egg whites at high speed on handheld mixer till it forms soft peaks, two to three minutes or so. Set them aside.

To prepare cupcakes, soft flour, baking powder, corn starch & kosher salt together in large mixing bowl. Set it aside.

Use handheld mixer with paddle attachment affixed and beat butter at high speed till creamy and smooth, one minute or so. Add sugar. Then, beat at high speed for three to four minutes till creamed together well. Add vanilla and egg yolk. Beat at med-high till combined well.

Set hand mixer speed on low. Add dry ingredient mixture in 3 additions and alternate whole milk between additions.

Fold 1/3 cup of strawberry puree, egg whites & chopped strawberries in cupcake batter. It should be a bit thick. Spoon the batter into cupcake liners. Then, fill them half way full.

Bake in 350F oven for 20-25 minutes, till top of cupcake springs back when touched gently. Allow them to cool in pan for five minutes. Transfer to rack to finish cooling and serve.

Quick Sticky Buns

These buns use a shortcut for the crust, so they are really easy to make. I love these sticky buns on Sunday mornings or holidays. They take a little over an hour, but the majority of the prep time is waiting for the dough to rise to make full, fluffy buns.

Servings: 8

Preparation Time: 1 hour 20 minutes

Ingredients:

- 2½ tbsp. unsalted butter
- ½ c. packed light brown sugar, divided
- 2 tbsp. light corn syrup
- 2 tsp. freshly squeezed lemon juice
- ½ c. coarsely chopped pecans
- 1 (8 oz.) can refrigerated crescent dough
- ¾ tsp. ground cinnamon

Instructions:

Preheat the oven to 375°F. Butter a 9-by-3-inch cake pan.

In a small saucepan over low heat, melt the butter. Whisk in ¼ cup of brown sugar, then add the corn syrup and lemon juice and whisk until blended. Increase the heat to medium and whisk the mixture until the sugar melts. Bring to a slow, rolling boil for 2 minutes. Pour the syrup evenly over the bottom of the prepared cake pan. Sprinkle with the pecans.

Unroll the dough on a floured surface; press the perforations together. Roll out the dough into an 8-by-12-inch rectangle. Sprinkle it with the remaining ¼ cup of brown sugar and the cinnamon. Starting at the short side of the dough rectangle, roll up the dough. Cut the rolled-up dough crosswise into 8 (1-inch thick) rounds. Arrange the dough rounds, cut side down, in the pan with the syrup, spacing them evenly. Cover the pan with plastic wrap. Set it aside in a warm, draft-free area (a closed oven works great) to rise for about 45 minutes, until doubled in size.

Bake the buns in the preheated oven for about 20 minutes, until golden brown. Let them cool in the pan for 1 minute. Place a plate over the pan, invert the buns onto the plate, and lift the pan from the buns. Spoon any syrup remaining in the pan onto the buns and serve.

Chocolate Coconut Bars

These sweet yet hearty bars use coconut flour to make them gluten-free. They have an indulgent chocolate flavor that's complemented by coconut.

Servings: 16

Preparation Time: 35 minutes

Ingredients:

- 1½ c. coconut flour
- 1¼ c. quick-cooking rolled oats
- ¾ c. coconut sugar
- ½ c. unsweetened dark cocoa
- 2 tsp. baking soda
- 1 tsp. cinnamon
- 1 tsp. salt
- ½ tsp. baking powder
- ½ c. dark chocolate chips
- 3 large eggs
- ½ c. coconut butter/manna
- ½ c. coconut oil
- 1 tsp. vanilla extract
- ¾ c. water (if too dry)

Instructions:

Preheat the oven to 350°F. Grease a 13-by-9-inch pan.

In a large mixing bowl, combine the coconut flour, rolled oats, coconut sugar, cocoa, baking soda, cinnamon, salt, and baking powder and stir until well mixed. Fold in the chocolate chips.

In a small bowl, combine the eggs, coconut butter/manna, coconut oil, and vanilla. Using a hand mixer, or by hand, beat the mixture until well combined. Add it to the dry ingredients and mix well. If the mixture is too dry (very thin and clumping) slowly add enough water to make it moist and able to be stirred, until it's about the consistency of brownie batter. Pour the mixture into the prepared pan and press it into the corners.

Bake on the center rack in the preheated oven for 25 to 30 minutes. Let it cool, and then cut it into bars.

Salted Caramel Pear Pie

This is a delicious and unique pie. It is served cold, so it could even be made as a dessert. This impressive pie is a tasty combination of caramel and baked pears. I recommend making it with my *Caramel Sauce* for the best flavor, though you can also use a store-bought sauce as a shortcut if you must.

Servings: 4

Preparation Time: 1 hr. 10 minutes

Ingredients:

- 1 (2-count, 14 oz.) box refrigerated pie crusts
- 6 pears, peeled and cut into ½-inch pieces
- ¼ c. sugar, plus extra for sprinkling
- ¼ c. all-purpose flour
- 1 tsp. ground cinnamon
- 1 tbsp. freshly squeezed lemon juice
- 1 c. salted Caramel Sauce, divided
- 1 egg
- 1 tbsp. milk

Instructions:

Preheat the oven to 400°F.

Divide the box of pie crusts in half for one top crust and one bottom crust. Roll out one pie crust to a 12-inch circle using the directions on the box. Carefully place it in the bottom of a 9-by-2-inch pie dish. Make sure it is smooth.

In a medium mixing bowl, combine the pears, sugar, flour, cinnamon, and lemon juice. Stir until the pears are well coated. Spoon the filling into the pie dish, discarding any excess liquid in the bowl (the liquid will make your pie soggy). Drizzle ½ cup of the caramel sauce evenly across the top. Cover the pie dish with plastic wrap and place it in the refrigerator while you make the top crust.

Using the other half of the prepared pie crust, follow the package directions to roll it out and place it on top of the pie. Use a fork or sharp knife to prick holes in the top crust to allow ventilation. Beat the egg with the milk to create an egg wash. Lightly brush the top of the pie crust with the egg wash and sprinkle the brushed crust with sugar.

Place the pie on a large baking sheet. Bake on the center rack of the preheated oven for 20 minutes. Then, use a pie crust shield or place strips of aluminum foil over the edges of the pie crust to prevent them from burning. Reduce the temperature to 350°F and bake for an additional 35 minutes, or until the pie crust is golden brown.

Allow the pie to cool for 3 hours at room temperature before serving. Drizzle the slices of pie with the remaining caramel sauce and serve.

S'more Sundae

This is the perfect dessert to serve on a hot summer night. This decadent dessert tastes like a campfire treat. If you don't want to use the broiler to melt the marshmallows, you can toast them over the open flame of a gas stove using metal—not flammable wooden! — skewers.

Servings: 1

Preparation Time: 6 minutes

Ingredients:

- 1 graham cracker
- 3 scoops fudge swirl ice cream
- 2 tbsps. chocolate syrup
- 10 mini marshmallows

Instructions:

Set the oven to broil. Line a rimmed baking sheet with aluminum foil.

Put the graham cracker in a zip-top bag and crush until the texture resembles fine crumbs.

Scoop the ice cream into a bowl, drizzle with chocolate syrup and sprinkle crushed graham crackers on top.

Put the mini marshmallows on the prepared baking sheet. Transfer the baking sheet to the oven and broil for 30 seconds to 1 minute, until the marshmallows start to turn golden. Remove from the oven.

Carefully place the marshmallows on top of the sundae and serve.

Microwave Potato Chips

This is a super easy recipe for chips. It is great to make for a snack or you can even serve them with dinner. These potato chips are so light and crispy that it's hard to believe they're made in the microwave.

Servings: 2

Preparation Time: 20 minutes

Ingredients:

- 1 russet potato
- 2 tbsp. olive oil
- 1 tsp. table salt

Instructions:

Fill a large bowl about halfway with ice, then add cold water to about 2 inches below the top of the bowl.

Scrub the potato to remove any dirt from the skin. Potatoes grow in the ground, so make sure you're getting any dirt out of the eyes. Using a knife, cut the potatoes as thin as you can. If possible, the potato slices should be almost transparent. Quickly submerge each potato slice in the ice water. This will keep the potatoes from turning grayish or pink. Let the potato slices soak in the ice water for at least 5 minutes.

Place a piece of parchment paper on a microwave-safe plate.

Working in batches, remove enough potato slices from the water to cover the plate in a single layer. Leave the remaining potato slices in the water until you are ready to cook them.

Use paper towels to dry the potato slices and arrange them on the plate so they are not touching.

Brush each potato slice with a light coating of olive oil and sprinkle lightly with salt. Microwave on high for 2 minutes, 30 seconds.

Using oven mitts or pot holders, carefully remove the plate from the microwave.

Using tongs, flip the potato chips over.

Return the potatoes to the microwave and cook on high for 2 more minutes, or until golden brown. The timing may vary based on your microwave. If the potato chips are not golden brown after 2 minutes, continue to cook in 30-second increments until the potato chips are golden.

Sprinkle the chips lightly with salt while still hot.

Repeat with the remaining potato slices.

Maple Granola with Cranberries

This recipe is great for breakfast or as a snack. It uses almonds and cranberries to add flavor and texture. Once you learn how to make granola at home and realize how cheap and easy it is, you'll never have to buy it again.

Servings: 6

Preparation Time: 1 hour 25 minutes

Ingredients:

- Nonstick cooking spray, for coating the baking sheets
- 3 c. gluten-free rolled oats
- 1 c. raw slivered almonds
- 1 c. raw walnuts
- ¾ c. coconut flakes or shredded coconut
- ¼ c. plus 2 tbsps. light brown sugar
- 3 tbsp. ground flaxseed (optional)
- 1 tsp. ground cinnamon
- ¾ tsp. table salt
- ¼ c. plus 2 tbsps. maple syrup
- ¼ c. canola oil, olive oil, or coconut oil
- 1 tsp. vanilla extract
- ½ c. dried cranberries

Instructions:

Preheat the oven to 250°F.

Line 2 rimmed baking sheets with aluminum foil and spray with nonstick cooking spray.

In a large bowl, combine the oats, almonds, walnuts, coconut, brown sugar, flaxseed (if using), cinnamon, and salt.

In a small bowl, combine the maple syrup, canola oil, and vanilla. Whisk together a bit so it's one uniform mixture.

Stir the syrup mixture into the oat mixture and keep stirring until the oats are coated. You can use your hands if you think it'll give you a better sense of when the oats are evenly coated.

Evenly divide the mixture onto both prepared baking sheets, making sure to spread it into an even layer.

Transfer the baking sheets to the oven and bake for about 1 hour 15 minutes, or until the granola looks toasty brown and smells delicious. Stir it using a spatula every 20 minutes as it's baking. Remove from the oven.

Evenly divide the dried cranberries between both baking sheets. Using a spatula, press them into the granola mixture.

Let the granola cool completely. Break it apart and store it in an airtight container for up to 2 weeks.

Apple Fritters

These apple fritters are perfect for breakfast or as a snack. They taste like the ones you would get at a fair, but this recipe is easier to make.

Preparation Time: 45 Minutes

Servings: 20

Ingredients

- 2 c. all-purpose flour
- 1/4 c. white sugar
- 1 tbsp. baking powder
- 1/2 tsp. ground nutmeg
- 1 tsp. salt
- 2 eggs
- 1 c. milk
- 2 quarts oil for deep frying
- 4 large apples, peeled and cored
- 1/2 c. confectioners' sugar for dusting

Instructions:

Combine salt, flour, nutmeg, baking powder, and sugar in a medium bowl.

Whisk milk and eggs together in another bowl. Combine the two bowls of mixture together until smooth.

Pour oil in a skillet, deep fryer, or deep pot; heat to 190°C (375°F). Cut apples into half-inch rings. Submerge sliced apples in batter and fry in batches until golden, flip once.

Place on paper towels to drain. Sprinkle confectioners' sugar on top.

Banana Fritters

These are an easy and yummy dessert. They can be served with syrup or powdered sugar.

Preparation Time: 45 Minutes

Servings: 10

Ingredients:

- 2 quarts oil for frying
- 1 c. all-purpose flour
- 1 1/4 tsps. baking powder
- 1/4 tsp. salt
- 1 egg, beaten
- 2 c. milk
- 2 tsps. canola oil
- 3 bananas, mashed
- 1 tbsp. lemon juice
- 2 tbsps. confectioners' sugar

Instructions:

Pour oil in a deep fryer, heat to 190°C (375°F).

Combine salt, baking powder, and flour in a big bowl.

Beat egg, canola oil, and milk in another medium-sized bowl; combine into the flour mixture. Fold in lemon juice and bananas.

Mix well and form into about 10 balls. Fry in hot oil for 5 minutes until slightly brown, work in batches.

Place on paper towels to drain. Dust with confectioners' sugar on top.

Conclusion

Healthy eating for teens is quite similar to that of young children. You just have to roll up your sleeves and change the recipes to suit their needs.

The best way to make sure your kids and teens eat healthily is to start early. Remember that a child yearns for what he is fed the most often. There are many healthy recipes for children and teens that will always be successful. Your children will surely thank you for it.

If you are cooking for yourself, it can be a real pain to have to constantly be digging through recipes and trying to figure out what goes with what. This cookbook is here to make your life easier. Not only does it have tons of recipes that are easy to make, but each recipe is sorted by the type of meal it makes, so if you want to make something sweet, you do not have to find the page that has desserts on it. Instead, you will just go to the page with all of the desserts and pick out whichever one looks best. The next time you want to cook something for yourself or for your family, be sure to remember this book as a resource.

Enjoy the recipes with your family and friends! Thank you so much!

Author's Afterthoughts

With so many books out there to choose from, I want to thank you for choosing this one and taking precious time out of your life to buy and read my work. Readers like you are the reason I take such passion in creating these books.

It is with gratitude and humility that I express how honored I am to become a part of your life and I hope that you take the same pleasure in reading this book as I did in writing it.

Can I ask one small favour? I ask that you write an honest and open review on Amazon of what you thought of the book. This will help other readers make an informed choice on whether to buy this book.

My sincerest thanks,

Angel Burns

If you want to be the first to know about news, new books, events and giveaways, subscribe to my newsletter by clicking the link below

https://angel-burns.gr8.com

or Scan QR-code

Printed in Great Britain
by Amazon